Stones in the Bloody Stream

Copyright © 2005 by Seth E. Frank
All Rights Reserved

© NEW EDEN PRESS, 2005
ISBN 960-88450-1-7

First edition

Seth E. Frank

Stones in the Bloody Stream

Remembrances of War and Terrorism

NEW EDEN PRESS

To Aliki Perroti,
A healing voice amidst the din of war and violence

Contents

The April Hill 13
The Vietnam War Memorial 17
Home from the War 21

ELEGY FOR THE WORLD TRADE CENTER
WTC Lament 25
Voice of a Victim: In Transit 29
Postscript to a Tragedy 31
Baltimore 33

Dialogue with the Oracle 41
Jihad 43

The April Hill

Soon I will climb again the April hill,
As first I did when all the daffodils
Were ablaze with the fire of a morning sun
That melted a fortnight's icy chill.
Because of when I saw those daffodils
I called it then and since the April hill.

Sometimes when I'd visit the April hill
I'd share it with only a whippoorwill,
Whose song in my ear would guide my eye,
Beneath a brightly burnished twilight sky,
Along rocky ridges and mossy rills
To the heart of the glen where my mind
Would refresh and my soul would refill.

One night I led you up the April hill,
Wearing my military khaki twills.
We cavorted wildly on the fertile ground
  without regard to cost,
Found much more than you feared you lost
And in the finding caused more than wine to spill.

They sent me overseas, far from the April hill.
With fresh memories of our ecstatic thrills
I wrote to you from old world foxholes,
  desert defilades and tropical tents
And told you all my feelings and events.
But your response was heartbreakingly nil.

Then on an island where soldiers fought and killed,
On one of that island's nameless numbered hills
The fire that blazed was not from daffodils,
The pain in flesh writhing on the earth
Was not the pain of giving birth,
But of the abattoir that was that shameless hill.

I'm ready now to climb the April hill,
The caisson's polished to a fare-thee-well,
The musket's loaded, the flag's unfurled,
The bugler's poised on my beloved hill,
Where I shall be forever happy and forever still.

And I shall wait with patience and good will,
For the child I did not live to see,
The child conceived by you and me
That passionate night upon the hill,
To come and lay upon my simple grave
Handfuls of lovely April daffodils.

The Vietnam War Memorial

You must run your fingers over the names
That are chiseled in stone, the names of the dead
Whose touch brings them to life in the mind's eye,
A miracle like braille that lifts the veil
On slumbering treasures of memory:

The etched letters of his family name,
So familiar, called often by teachers
In many school classes over the years:
His responses ranged from first rate knowledge
To sometimes unprepared, taking the hit
For having been a good Samaritan
On and off the campus, helping others
At his own expense with no time for sleep,
Let alone to prepare the assignment.
He had character with a capital "C".

Elsewhere the name of another good friend.
We shared the field for many sports events.
The choice of all for captain of the team,
His skill and spirit led and inspired us:
Passing the ball back and forth between us
On the basketball court and joining at the hoop;
In baseball, "Throw it to me. We've caught him
Stealing. He'll be out by a country mile."
Celebrating with bear hugs and high fives,
Not knowing the bells of Edgar Allan Poe
And of John Donne would toll before their time.

More recalled than classes and athletics:
Good fellowship, firm friendship, one for all,
Morning coffees, social evenings, week-ends
At one another's homes, pizza and beer,
Late night bull sessions, light and heavy talk,
Secrets and confidences, still respected,
Career and marriage plans, interrupted
By the war...

United by love of country,
Young stalks of golden grain were cut down by swords
That fate had failed to beat into ploughshares,
Felled in a flash on strange and hostile soil,
The best and bravest of their generation.

Between the blood stained bookends of tragedy
The youth that burned brightly with passion and promise
Is memorialized now in stony silence
With more than fifty-eight thousand scattered souls.
Run your fingers again over their names
Chiseled here in stone, the names of these dead.
Speak to them and listen as they speak to you:
A dialogue between fallen heroes
And the citizens they died to protect.
Comfort the families who mourn their dead.
And remember we are all one family:
Mothers, fathers, sisters, brothers and friends.

Stepping back from the wall of black granite
The images fade and the veil descends.

A day may come, after our time has passed,
When this stately, handsome memorial
May crumble from indifference, catastrophe
Or other unkind cause and be dissolved
In dust, as are those whose lives it honors.

*This poem was inspired by Senator John Kerry
and my acquaintance with his friend
Lt. Richard Warren Pershing who was killed in Vietnam.
The characters and events recalled are entirely imagined.*

Home From The War

Mother, mother, do not grieve.
To your bosom let me cleave,
Share your warmth and wisdom, please
And persuade you not to grieve.

As the bees home to their hive,
As the harvest moon arrives,
Listen as the clock strikes five:
The dead poets come alive.

Hear them sing you songs of love,
As to you my father proved
When together in Pan's grove
You embraced and kissed and roved.

  (When their songs have all been sung,
    The poets retire, one by one.)

Saintly mother, do not pine.
Everything will turn out fine.
Like a cat my lives are nine.
I've used but one, dear mother mine.

Farewell, mother, I must leave.
Though I feel your bosom heave,
Please don't weep and please don't grieve
Your son laid out in bloody sleeves.

Elegy For The World Trade Center
Dedicated to the Victims and to Mayor Rudy Giuliani

WTC Lament

Tuesday was a sunny morning
Hope was in the sky.
Who knew in the day's bright dawning
Thousands soon would die?

People went about their business
Doing what they do.
Till acts of unholy terror
Split the world in two.

Tall and stately stood the towers
Like a bride and groom.
Then two jet planes crashed the party
Heralding their doom.

Ring around ye lads and lassies,
Sing a song of pain.
Cry as down each tower crashes
Never seen again.

The City's force of red and blue
In instant motion
Bravely undertook the rescue.
Salute now the many, sad but true,
Who gave their last full measure of devotion.

All join hands dear lads and lassies,
Mourn the bloody stain.
Swear to each dead soul that passes,
"You've not died in vain."

Courage, lads, and courage, lassies.
Raise Old Glory high.
Even in the burning ashes
Freedom will not die.

Lay your wreaths and light your candles.
Life's forever changed.
Curse the dark, but catch the vandals
Horribly deranged.

Tuesday was a sunny morning,
But such a sad and solemn night.

In memoriam for September 11th

Voice Of A Victim: In Transit
July 1, 1950 - September 11, 2001

Four score and seven years after Gettysburg
My family took a ferry from lower Manhattan,
  Blessed then with fresh breezes and clean air,
To Hoboken, there to board the Erie Lackawana Railroad
  bound for Pennsylvania.

As the blackened iron locomotive
Belched and bruited its way down the track
Soot and smoke filled the atmosphere
And cinders nested in my eyes,
Causing them to tear like the Johnstown Flood,
While I struggled to glimpse the sky.

Time buried those moments with many others
And the waters of Lethe washed away their memory
  Until...

I am again in lower Manhattan,
Surrounded by soot and smoke,
Far from fresh breezes and clean air.
Once more cinders nest in my eyes,
Drowned in blood and tears,
Unable to glimpse the sky
As I lie in a measureless bed
  of burning ash and putrefaction,
Silent and still, with twisted steel for a winding sheet.

I wait, as before, for the ferry to take me to New Jersey
  across the Hudson, transformed now into the River Styx.
I do not think in Hoboken I will board the train
  to Pennsylvania.

But somewhere, in Manhattan or New Jersey
  or possibly even Pennsylvania,
The President will speak and give the people
  comfort and resolve,
As another did once at Gettysburg.

Postscript To A Tragedy

September, not April, is the
 cruelest month.
Auden, not Eliot, was right:
"The unmentionable odour
 of death
Offends the September night."

BALTIMORE

I went to Baltimore early this November.
The sixth to be exact, Election Day.
Another bright Tuesday like the beginning of that earlier one.
Though this one had nothing to do with the other in my mind.
I went with no purpose of my own
   but to accompany someone who goes annually
   for check-ups at Johns Hopkins,
   Baltimore's legendary temple of health care.

I looked forward to my visit and dwelt on seeing pleasant things:
   The harbor, the site where the Star Spangled Banner
   was composed,
   the well known row houses, perhaps one
   with a plaque commemorating
   Edgar Allan Poe (as New York has at the corner of Ann
     and Nassau Streets),
   or Babe Ruth's or Russell Baker's boyhood home;
   H.L. Mencken's various haunts, Johns Hopkins itself of course
   and maybe even Camden Yards,
   the new model baseball stadium —
   all the pride of Baltimore.

Anticipating these, I was wholly unprepared,
   as I walked from the train toward the exit of the station,
for the Amtrak Memorial to the New York World Trade Center:
   A microcosm of that colossal wreckage — twisted steel girders
   and fractured stones, ash and dust, strewn
   with a crushed and crusted fireman's helmet,
   workers' locker key plates, electrical conduit . . .
   and additions by unknown mourners
    of pictures of missing persons,
   cards of remembrance, poems . . .
   all encircled with a photographic ring
   of rescue efforts amidst the rubble.
Joe Louis and all the other great heavyweight boxing champions
   could not have hit me with a more arresting blow.

I am not a mathematician.
But I believe that a similar memorial
Could be erected in every large and small city of the world.
And still there would be enough material left
To replace them all each year
Throughout this sorry new Millennium.

THE CITY OF NEW YORK
OFFICE OF THE MAYOR
NEW YORK, N.Y. 10007

November 30, 2001

Mr. Seth E. Frank
LeBoeuf, Lamb, Greene & MacRae L.L.P.
125 West 55th Street
New York, NY 10019

Dear Mr. Frank:

    I write to thank you for your lovely poems. It was very kind of you to send them and I very much appreciate your support during this most difficult time.

    Best wishes.

Sincerely,

Rudolph W. Giulinai
Mayor

THE WHITE HOUSE

WASHINGTON

June 28, 2002

Mr. Seth E. Frank
12th Floor
125 West 55th Street
New York, New York 10019-5369

Dear Mr. Frank:

Thank you for writing about the acts of war committed against the United States on September 11 and for sending your thoughtful remembrance. In the face of this evil, our country remains strong and united, a beacon of freedom and opportunity to the rest of the world.

Our government continues to serve the American people. Our intelligence, military, and law enforcement communities are working non-stop to find those responsible for these attacks. We will make no distinction between the terrorists who committed these acts and those who help or harbor them.

We must remember that our Arab and Muslim American citizens love our Nation and must be treated with dignity and respect. Americans of every creed, ethnicity, and national origin must unite against our common enemies.

Since these terrible tragedies occurred, our citizens have been generous, kind, resourceful, and brave. I encourage all Americans to find a way to help. Web sites like LibertyUnites.org can serve as a resource for those wanting to participate in the relief efforts.

May God bless you and may God bless America.

Sincerely,

George W. Bush

Dialogue With The Oracle

Tell me, please, o wise one,
Why are all the oceans rising?
Is it 'cause the party's over
   and the ice caps fast are melting?
No, my son, it is because the gods are crying
   that so many helpless creatures
   needlessly are dying.

Jihad

We westerners are learning Islamic
Words and tenets much more quickly than we
Ever thought we would and faster than we
Came to taste middle eastern food and drink.
"Jihad" we find on good authority
Comes straight from the Koran and means "striving".
But in the minds and mouths of fanatic
Terrorists how distressingly distorted
It's been twisted into war, violence,
Death and destruction, like some misshapen beast
Resurrected from the festering pits of hell.

I read in the *The New Yorker* magazine
   of January 21, 2002
On facing pages 32 and 33: a poignant poem
About love ending and family life
Surviving on the left page and on the right
The dread fate of mujahideen captured
By the Taliban who first were beaten
Until half dead, then had their hearts and eyes
Cut out and at last were hanged upside down.
And I think: What place can poetry have
In a world of such stark brutality?

After the deadly perversion done to it
"Jihad" will be as toxic and abhorred
As "Chernobyl"; and for at least as long
May not find a welcome on western tongues.
Perhaps there's little cause to mourn the loss
Of a single unfamiliar foreign word
Compared to the uncounted people's lives
Which end unnoticed, let alone unsung.

But as a profound poet said centuries ago,
"Each man's death diminishes me."
So we must strive,
   hand in hand with all our global brethren,
As hope alone, of course, will never do,
   to make a world that's safe
For the entire human family:
A world renewed, resolved and unafraid;
A world that has again a decent place for poetry.

Acknowledgments

I would like to thank Randall Warner for her professional advice and assistance and for generously sharing the experience derived from her lengthy career in publishing; and Simos Saltiel for his artistic design and supervision of production. Without them this book would not have been possible. I also wish to thank my secretary Marie Witcher who typed these poems from my indecipherable script, probably never dreaming, anymore than I, that one day they would appear in a book.

THE BOOK *STONES IN THE BLOODY STREAM: REMEMBRANCES OF WAR AND TERRORISM*, BY SETH E. FRANK WAS DESIGNED BY RED CREATIVE AND PRINTED IN 500 COPIES USING GARAMOND CLASSIC 11.5 PTS ON 130 GR CHAGALL NEVE PAPER AT GIORGOS SKORDOPOULOS PRINTERS THESSALONIKI GREECE IN JANUARY 2005 ILLUSTRATION BY VIKTOR MOSCHOPOULOS